UNDERSTANDING "SPIRITUALS"

ANOINTING WITH OIL

ANOINTING WITH OIL

EASTWOOD ANABA

ISBN: 978-9988-1-7319-7

Request for information should be addressed to:
The Administrator
Desert Leaf Publications
P. O. Box 299
Bolgatanga, UER, Ghana, W/A
Tel: +233-3820-23077
E-mail: info@eastwoodanaba.com
Website: www.eastwoodanaba.com

Edited by: Arrow Editing Services
P. O. Box 3298, Accra, Ghana
mayford78@gmail.com
Tel: +233244548296

Design & Production
DESIGN SOLUTIONS
Tel: +1905-216 2653
E-mail: georgepabi@yahoo.com
sarpongpabi@yahoo.ca

Printed in Gt. Britain by Polestar Wheatons

CONTENTS

INTRODUCTION

U sing anointing oil to minister to people is a controversial issue among believers. Some believers detest its use so much that they walk out of meetings when it is used. The aim of this book is to give us biblical insight into the purpose of the anointing oil and how it can be used for the edification and blessing of believers. With regard to this subject we don't have to condemn others for their position.

It is scriptural to use anointing oil in ministration but not mandatory. The law of liberty allows those whose faith is enhanced by the use of the oil to use it and those whose faith does not require it not to use it. Those who use it are not more spiritual than those who don't use it and those who don't use it don't necessarily have more faith in the Word of God than those who use it.

We know from the Scriptures that symbols and tokens are used in the operations of the Holy Ghost and oil is one of those symbols. It is used on people as a sign of the Holy Ghost coming upon them and working in them. It can be rubbed or poured on them to symbolise various activities of the Holy Ghost.

The use of anointing oil occurs in both the New and Old Testaments. God instituted its use in the Old Testament for activities such as anointing kings, priests, preparing offerings, anointing the instruments of the Tabernacle and providing lights for the Tabernacle.

And thou shalt anoint Aaron and his sons, and consecrate them, that they may minister unto me in the priest's office.

And thou shalt speak unto the children of Israel, saying, This shall be an holy anointing oil unto me throughout your generations.

Upon man's flesh shall it not be poured, neither shall ye make any other like it, after the composition of it: it is holy, and it shall be holy unto you.

Exodus 30:30-32

The anointing oil was so special that it was to come upon "no man's flesh." This means the special anointing oil for the priests was not supposed to touch ordinary people. Since the oil was poured on Aaron and his sons, the term "no man", could not have been in reference to every man but to those who had no covenant with God. The oil was dedicated to God for holy application throughout all the generations of the Jews. It must be noted that the phrase "throughout all your generations" referred to the Jewish Tabernacle and Temple of worship and not New Testament worship in Spirit and in truth.

One may ask why there is no burning of incense in the New Testament Church though God directed that incense should be burnt in the Tabernacle "throughout the generations" of the Israelites.

And Aaron shall burn thereon sweet incense every morning: when he dresseth the lamps, he shall burn incense upon it.

And when Aaron lighteth the lamps at even, he shall burn incense upon it, a perpetual incense before the LORD throughout your generations.

Exodus 30:7-8

Those who are opposed to the use of the anointing oil in church may jump at the above scriptural reference and say that if believers don't endorse the burning of incense today, they should not also practice the use of the anointing oil. The Scriptures are however, clear on the fact that the use of oil by New Testament saints is scriptural whereas the use of incense is not.

There are a few references to incense in the New

Testament but they don't suggest in any way that we use incense today. The book of Revelation likens incense to the prayer of the saints.

And when he had taken the book, the four beasts and four and twenty elders fell down before the Lamb, having every one of them harps, and golden vials full of odours, which are the prayers of saints.

Revelation 5:8

And the smoke of the incense, which came with the prayers of the saints, ascended up before God out of the angel's hand.

Revelation 8:4

The smoke of the incense was a symbol for prayer – the smoke accompanied the prayer of the saints. The Bible, however, does not say anywhere in the New Testament that Jesus or His disciples burned incense in the places where they prayed or accompanied their prayers with incense. Since the practices of Jesus Christ and the Apostles form the standard for New Testament practice, believers of today don't use incense in the practising of their faith.

A careful look at the occurrences of oil and incense show clearly that oil is of a wider application in the Bible than incense. The general use of oil in Jewish and other cultures makes it logical for it to

9

be used as a symbol of the Holy Ghost. Incense is not in common use like oil and its use as a symbol for spiritual things is not as widespread as oil. Oil, water, rain, fire and wind are easily identified with the Holy Ghost as symbols.

The anointing oil is for all generations of worshippers including New Testament saints. We are a royal priesthood and God has anointed us with the Holy Ghost. The anointing oil is a symbol of the spiritual anointing we have received from God.

> *But ye are a chosen generation, a royal priesthood, an holy nation, a peculiar people; that ye should shew forth the praises of him who hath called you out of darkness into his marvellous light:*
>
> *1 Peter 2:9*

God does not fill unbelievers with the Holy Ghost just as the anointing oil in the Tabernacle was not to be put on "any man". The oil was not put on individuals or groups of people whom God had not called or chosen. The anointing oil was to be used throughout all generations. It is a symbolic representation of the Holy Ghost who abides with the Church forever. To understand how the anointing oil works, we have to understand who the Holy Ghost is. Those who don't know the person of the Holy Ghost abuse and overemphasise the use of the anointing oil and subvert the faith of others with unethical practices.

CHAPTER 1

THE HOLY GHOST AND THE OIL

God gives the gift of the Holy Ghost to believers to indwell them and empower them to live victoriously and to do the work of ministry. Jesus referred to Him as "another Comforter" whom God would send in His place while He was physically absent from the Church.

> And I will pray the Father, and he shall give you another Comforter, that he may abide with you for ever;
> Even the Spirit of truth; whom the world cannot receive, because it seeth him not, neither knoweth him: but ye know him; for he dwelleth with you, and shall be in you.
>
> John 14:16-17

The Greek word for "another" is **allos**, which means another of the same kind. It is different from the Greek word **heteros**, which means a different thing altogether. The Holy Ghost has the same character as Jesus and operates in the same power Jesus has. Jesus promised us the person of the Holy Ghost. On the day of Pentecost, vials of oil did not drop from heaven but the person of the Holy Ghost did. The wind and the fire that showed up on that day were symbols of the Holy Ghost and not Himself.

The anointing oil in the Old Testament was for all the generations of the Jews until the coming of the Holy Ghost. When the Bible says in Exodus 30:31 that the holy anointing oil shall be unto God throughout generations of the Jews, it meant the physical anointing oil shall be indispensable until the coming of Christ and the Holy Ghost. It is the Holy Ghost who abides with the Church forever and not physical anointing oil.

There is no doubt that the anointing oil is an emblem of the Holy Ghost and we should not become over dependent on it as New Testament believers. What the oil was to Old Testament saints, the Holy Ghost is to New Testament saints. The question however, remains as to whether after the coming down and indwelling of the Holy Ghost in New Testament believers, they should still anoint themselves with physical oil.

The Bible mentions instances in the New

Testament where physical anointing oil was used in ministration. This means that it is scriptural to use the anointing oil. Believers who use the anointing oil must however, be careful not to overemphasise its use since it is a symbol of the Holy Ghost and not the Holy Ghost Himself.

Some people who use oil in ministration insist it must be olive oil and no other kind of oil. The anointing oil is a symbol of the Holy Ghost and we should not be too legalistic about the type of oil that is used. In the Old Testament the anointing oil used in the Tabernacle was pure Olive oil compounded with spices. However, the Olive tree is not of universal occurrence and it is not possible to use it in all situations, in all places.

The requirement for oil to be used is to make sure the oil one uses has the properties that adequately portray the Holy Ghost such as purity, fluidity and brilliance. Olive oil is pale yellow to greenish in colour when it is in its pure state. The pure nature of the oil points to the holy nature of the Holy Ghost. Its fluidity speaks about the flow of the power of the Holy Ghost and the brilliance of its colour alludes to His glory.

The Bible mentions the use of oil in the ministry of our Lord Jesus Christ when He sent His disciples to preach the gospel, heal the sick and cast out

14

devils. The sick and the oppressed were anointed with oil and were healed.

And they went out, and preached that men should repent.

And they cast out many devils, and anointed with oil many that were sick, and healed them.

Mark 6:12-13

The disciples of Jesus anointed the sick with oil and healed them. The application of the oil was not a customary or cosmetic thing. It was an integral part of the healing of the sick. The Bible says, "And they cast out many devils, and anointed with oil many that were sick, and healed them." When we apply oil on the sick our faith should not be in the oil but in the holiness, power and glory of the Holy Ghost.

The Apostle James directed the believers to pray over the sick and anoint them with oil in the name of the Lord and the prayer of faith would heal them.

Is any sick among you? let him call for the elders of the church; and let them pray over him, anointing him with oil in the name of the Lord:

And the prayer of faith shall save the sick, and the Lord shall raise him up; and if he have committed sins, they shall be forgiven him.

James 5:14-15

This Scripture reference states clearly that the Early Church used oil in ministration to the sick. The use of oil is not just an Old Testament practice but a New Testament one as well. With regard to the New Testament mention of the use of oil in the book of James, some people believe that James directed its use because he was a Jew. We must not miss the fact that the Holy Ghost inspired James to write about the use of anointing oil. The Holy Ghost dictated his beliefs and not Jewish tradition. Many factors relating to healing are mentioned in James 5:14-15 such as the elders of the church, prayer, the name of the Lord and faith. These factors are both Old Testament and New Testament factors and so the anointing oil is also an Old Testament and New Testament thing.

Elders should anoint afflicted and sick believers and pray for them to be healed. Note that it is not just the oil that heals the sick but the other factors in the prayer. It is the authority (the Name of Jesus) behind the oil that counts. It is the activity behind the oil (the prayer) that counts. It is the force behind the oil (faith in the Lord) that counts. It is the human instruments behind the oil (the elders) that counts.

In September 1994, a sister approached me in London with a disease. Her body had been itching almost every minute for five months. I anointed her with oil on the face and prayed the prayer of faith. The next day, I travelled to Hamburg. After three days, in a telephone conversation, she said the itching ceased immediately after the prayer and had not come back. After two weeks she confirmed that she had been totally healed without the slightest symptom persisting.

Many people who misunderstand the use of symbols and tokens actually fail to explore God's abundant channels of blessing. They are therefore limited in ministry. There are people who argue that the anointing oil should be used only in cases of healing. Such people ignore the fact that in Mark 6:13, the Bible says they cast out devils and anointed the sick with oil. The devils had something to do with the sicknesses. After casting out the devils, the sick were anointed and healed and possibly consecrated to the Lord against any further attacks of demons. Demons cause many discomforts and hurts in people's lives apart from sickness and anointing them with oil in prayer provides a barrier against demonic attacks.

A few years ago, I went to preach in a West African country called Togo. One night during my ministration, a woman walked to the platform and touched my feet. Initially, I thought she touched me as a point of contact to receive the impartation of the anointing. On the contrary, after a few seconds

I felt an uncomfortable sensation in my right foot and I discerned that the woman had released a demonic deposit into my foot. On my return home I continued to feel pain and discomfort in the foot. I prayed over it and wiped it with oil and the pain left almost instantly.

The reference to the oil in the book of James is insightful. It makes a strong case for using the anointing oil for situations other than the healing of the sick. This reference mentions many factors like elders of the church, prayer, the name of the Lord and faith. Elders of the church engage in other activities such as teaching and governing the church. Prayer brings deliverance and supplies our needs. The name of the Lord is the key to the casting out of devils and walking in the supernatural power of God. Faith is the indispensable spiritual disposition without which no man can please the Lord. If these factors are versatile in operation, we cannot limit the anointing oil which is mentioned in the same context in James 5:14 to just healing.

When elders pray and anoint the sick with oil, the prayer of faith saves the sick person, the Lord raises him up and if he has committed sins, they are forgiven him. If someone is not sick and needs to be raised up in life, prayer and anointing with oil is a means of raising him up. The application of the anointing oil during prayer releases the presence of the Holy Ghost, which causes conviction that results in the confession of sin, repentance, and forgiveness of sin. This is the reason why James said if the sick person has committed any sins they shall be forgiven him.

I had an interesting experience in a church that goes to prove the power of anointing people with oil besides cases that require healing. A gentleman joined a group of people who needed ministration. His condition was one of alopecia – partial baldness on the head. I poured some oil on his head and prayed for him. The following year when I went back to the same church to minister he testified to the restoration of his hair.

Besides anointing the sick, the anointing oil serves numerous purposes as seen in the anointing oil in the Tabernacle. The use of the anointing oil in the Gospel according to Saint Mark and the Epistle of James is proof that it is scriptural though not compulsory for believers to use oil in ministration. If holy men and women of God use the anointing oil, the spiritual benefits are uncountable. Oil in the hands of unbelieving pretenders only gives demons an emollient effect to be comfortable. If a believer anoints the sick with oil but has no faith in God nothing happens.

We should not shy away from using the anointing oil with the excuse that fake preachers

use it. The existence of counterfeit money does not prevent us from using genuine money. Those who condemn the use of anointing oil because of its abuse by false preachers, forget that those they refer to as false preachers also use the Bible to preach. It is surprising that the genuine preachers don't discard their Bibles.

"False preachers" call their organisations "church", "ministry" and "chapel" and the "genuine ones" do the same. It is hypocritical to discard symbols and tokens with the excuse that false preachers abuse their usage. Occult groups did not invent the use of oil to anoint the sick. Some New Testament preachers, who reject the use of anointing oil with the claim that it is Old Testament practice, receive tithes without contending that it is an Old Testament practice. False preachers imitate the truth, distort and abuse it but true ministers of God must not give their godly inheritance to pretenders.

Having made the point that the anointing oil can be applied in many situations I wish to go back to the Old Testament and trace a few instances where the anointing oil was applied. The Scriptures don't tell us anywhere not to use the anointing oil in the way the Old Testament prophets and saints used it.

The law of liberty applies in the use of the

anointing oil and the Old Testament examples give us the guidelines for its general use. A casual look at the occurrences where anointing oil was used in the Old Testament shows that it was not used mainly for healing the sick and casting out devils. With the liberty of the Spirit however, Jesus' disciples and the Early Church used it for the healing of the sick. The combined scenarios give us the advantage today. We are at liberty to follow the Old Testament examples as well as the New Testament ones. God commanded Moses with strong words to anoint Aaron and his sons and set them apart for the work of the ministry. *"And thou shalt anoint Aaron and his sons ..."* was the command God gave Moses. In the next chapter, we shall study the use of the anointing oil in the service of the Tabernacle.

CHAPTER 2

AND THOU SHALT ANOINT ...

Besides anointing the sick with oil, the Scriptures show that oil was used to anoint people who were set apart for divine purposes. This was especially so for prophets, kings and priests. In the New Testament, the apostles laid hands on separated people and prayed over them with prophecy. The use of oil to consecrate people set apart for ministry is not stated in the New Testament. The history of the Church is however, characterised by the use of oil to anoint people who are called into various offices. The reason why it is biblical to use oil is because its use is not annulled in the New Testament.

God instructed Moses to anoint Aaron and his sons and consecrate them to minister to Him. He could have simply breathed on them to consecrate and empower them for the priesthood office but He instructed Moses to anoint them with oil. God does not do meaningless things and so the use of the anointing oil must be significant.

And thou shalt anoint Aaron and his sons, and consecrate them, that they may minister unto me in the priest's office.

And thou shalt speak unto the children of Israel, saying, This shall be an holy anointing oil unto me throughout your generations.

Exodus 30:30-31

The Hebrew word for "consecrate" is the word **qãdash**, which means "sanctify", "hallow" and "holy". By applying the oil, the holy nature of the Holy Ghost was imparted to Aaron and his sons and they could stand before God. It is more important to be holy in one's spirit and body than to pour drums of oil on one's head. When the anointing oil is applied, the Holy Ghost personally separates a man or woman unto Himself and imparts His holy nature to him or her.

Like the priests, kings were anointed to usher them into their office. The Prophet Samuel anointed Saul, king over Israel without any elections or a referendum. Walking in obedience to God's Word is the most important step to your promotion to a place of honour in life. It is however, not out of place to believe that after your obedience to God, the laying on of hands coupled with being anointed with oil contributes to the promotion you receive in life.

Then Samuel took a vial of oil, and poured it upon his head, and kissed him, and said, Is it not because the LORD hath anointed thee to be captain over his inheritance?

1 Samuel 10:1

There is no spiritual instrument for measuring the effect of the anointing on a person. Just as we cannot quantify the effect of anointing someone with oil, we cannot also dismiss its effect. The positive things we see in the believer's life are the result of the combination of the working of the Word of God, the infilling of the Holy Ghost, obedience to the Word of God, laying on of hands, anointing with oil, prayer, worship, giving of offerings and a host of other spiritual activities.

If some people refute the effects produced by the laying on of hands and being anointed with oil, others may also refute the effects of things like giving offerings and praying. We cannot attribute the blessings and miracles that take place in our lives to some particular spiritual activities and at the same time deny the efficacy of others. Atheists deny the existence of God while carnal believers are selective in the

spiritual things they choose to believe.

Anointing individuals with oil was not an impotent customary exercise in Israel. It was a spiritual process that had the power to install kings and replace them. Saul was put on the throne through the agency of the anointing and David replaced him through the same means.

And he sent, and brought him in. Now he was ruddy, and withal of a beautiful countenance, and goodly to look to. And the LORD said, Arise, anoint him: for this is he.

Then Samuel took the horn of oil, and anointed him in the midst of his brethren: and the Spirit of the LORD came upon David from that day forward. So Samuel rose up, and went to Ramah.

1 Samuel 16:12-13

Two things are mentioned in the above scripture reference, namely the anointing of David with oil and the coming of the Spirit of the LORD upon him. The latter followed the former – Samuel anointed David with oil and the Spirit of the LORD came upon him.

The Holy Ghost comes upon people when they are anointed with oil. The coming of the Holy Ghost upon people explains why they feel a cold or hot sensation and sometimes fall under

25

the power. The oil does not make them shake or fall – it is the Holy Ghost who makes those things happen.

God directed Elijah to anoint Jehu and Hazael as kings over Israel and Syria respectively and Elisha as a prophet in his place. This directive adds the prophets to the list of people who were put into their offices through the anointing.

And the LORD said unto him, Go, return on thy way to the wilderness of Damascus: and when thou comest, anoint Hazael to be king over Syria:

And Jehu the son of Nimshi shalt thou anoint to be king over Israel: and Elisha the son of Shaphat of Abelmeholah shalt thou anoint to be prophet in thy room.

I Kings 19:15-16

Elisha assumed his prophetic office by receiving Elijah's mantle. We don't know whether at any point Elijah anointed Elisha with oil. Whether Elisha received the anointing through being anointed with oil or receiving a mantle, the point is that God uses spiritual means to undertake His purposes. If we are sceptical about anointing a person with oil for empowerment, we are likely to doubt the impartation of the anointing through a mantle. God's methods don't always appeal to our logic but that is what makes Him God. It is impossible to find intelligent explanations to spiritual things.

Of the three individuals God asked Elijah to anoint, the Bible gives us a detailed narration of how the anointing oil was poured on Jehu's head to anoint him king over Israel. Elijah did not anoint Jehu directly but did it spiritually through his connection with Elisha, his spiritual son. Elisha sent one of his young prophets who is believed by some scholars to be Jonah the son of Amittai to anoint Jehu king.

So the young man, even the young man the prophet, went to Ramothgilead.

And when he came, behold, the captains of the host were sitting; and he said, I have an errand to thee, O captain. And Jehu said, Unto which of all us? And he said, To thee, O captain.

And he arose, and went into the house; and he poured the oil on his head, and said unto him, Thus saith the LORD God of Israel, I have anointed thee king over the people of the LORD, even over Israel.

2 Kings 9:4-6

Note that the above exercise is spiritual. The prophet who anointed Jehu did not preach a sermon to him to impart faith to his heart. It is wrong to

27

insist that believers must always preach the Word of God before they undertake spiritual exercises like laying hands on someone and anointing them with oil.

It is an act of spiritual dishonesty for believers to discount the role the anointing plays in their lives. If the anointing oil influenced the election of priests, kings and prophets, it must have some influence on businessmen, politicians, academicians, ministers and parents.

God instructed Moses saying *"And thou shalt anoint Aaron and his sons ..."* Apart from the human beings who were anointed, the instruction – *"And thou shalt anoint ..."* applied to the anointing of the Tabernacle of the congregation, the Ark of the Covenant, the table, the vessels, the candlestick and the altar. Moses anointed all of them with the holy anointing oil and separated them unto God.

And thou shalt anoint the tabernacle of the congregation therewith, and the ark of the testimony,

And the table and all his vessels, and the candlestick and his vessels, and the altar of incense,

And the altar of burnt offering with all his vessels, and the laver and his foot.

*And thou shalt sanctify them, that they may
be most holy: whatsoever toucheth them shall
be holy.*

Exodus 30:26-29.

Aaron and his sons were to be anointed together
with all the vessels and instruments. Sanctified men
must work with sanctified tools to glorify God. The
New Testament does not teach us to anoint things
with oil but it does not tell us not to anoint them
either. It is all right to anoint pulpits, pews, musical
instruments, office furniture, buildings and other
things, thus consecrating them with prayer for the
use of the Lord. Domestic things like cars, houses,
beds and others can also be anointed. God has
called us to liberty. Use your liberty while making
sure that you don't place a stumbling block in the
way of others. In God's dealings with me in the
ministry, I anoint the sick and people called into
various ministries. I also anoint instruments and
physical things with oil.

Before God told Moses in the Law to anoint
Aaron and his sons with oil, the Patriarch Jacob
poured oil on a stone and made a vow unto God.

*And he was afraid, and said, How dreadful is
this place! this is none other but the house of
God, and this is the gate of heaven.*
And Jacob rose up early in the morning, and

took the stone that he had put for his pillows, and set it up for a pillar, and poured oil upon the top of it.

And he called the name of that place Bethel: but the name of that city was called Luz at the first.

And Jacob vowed a vow, saying, If God will be with me, and will keep me in this way that I go, and will give me bread to eat, and raiment to put on,

So that I come again to my father's house in peace; then shall the LORD be my God:

And this stone, which I have set for a pillar, shall be God's house: and of all that thou shalt give me I will surely give the tenth unto thee.

Genesis 28:17-22

The memorial pillar Jacob set up and poured the oil on was a kind of altar. Today we don't have to pour oil on stones and make vows because our human spirits and bodies are the temples and altars of God. Oil should be poured on human beings to consecrate them to God and not on stones. Jesus said if human beings stopped shouting out His praise the stones would take their place (Luke 19:40). If human beings are available there is no need for stones. Believers constantly dedicate themselves to God and He uses ministers to pour the anointing oil on them to do exploits for the Kingdom of God. The

Apostle Paul admonished the Romans to present their bodies as living sacrifices to God.

> *I beseech you therefore, brethren, by the mercies of God, that ye present your bodies a living sacrifice, holy, acceptable unto God, which is your reasonable service.*
>
> *And be not conformed to this world: but be ye transformed by the renewing of your mind, that ye may prove what is that good, and acceptable, and perfect, will of God.*
>
> *Romans 12:1-2*

"And thou shalt anoint ...", is still an operational imperative to God's people as they consecrate themselves for the ministry and dedicate things to God. We forfeit several spiritual blessings when we legalistically practise the things that are in the Bible based on whether they are in the Old Testament or the New Testament. The things that are written in the Old Testament are not just stories to excite us or to act as a recipe for religious debate. They are written to be examples we should follow and learn from.

We cannot ignore the fact that the use of the anointing oil and other symbols and tokens raises many questions that need to be addressed. I don't pretend to have all the answers but in the next chapter, I will make an attempt to answer a few of the questions well-meaning believers ask about anointing people who need the touch of the Holy Ghost. Believers must approach the issue of the anointing with open minds if they want to receive revelation and instruction from God. Some sections of the Body of Christ are so dogmatic in their use of the anointing oil or its rejection that it is impossible for the Holy Ghost to teach them anything new.

CHAPTER 3

ANOINTING WITH DECORUM

The Apostle Paul's directive that all things be done decently and orderly applies to the use of the anointing oil. The anointing oil should be applied with decorum. Decorum is doing things in ways that conform to good taste and propriety. As much as possible the use of the anointing oil should bring edification to the Body of Christ instead of confusion and strife.

Some ministers and believers practise unethical and indecent things that put people off the use of the anointing oil. Such practices include anointing certain parts of the human body that are considered private, dropping or pouring oil into delicate parts of the body like the eyes and pouring huge quantities of oil on individuals until their clothes are soaked with the oil. When the anointing oil is applied to a decent part of the body it permeates the entire body and so one does not have to remove another person's clothes to anoint him or her. Acts of indecency can also be found in churches that regularly use the anointing oil as the carpets and floors are messed up with stains and patches created by the spilling of the oil. The Apostle Paul's words in 1 Corinthians 14:40 must guide us – "Let all things be done decently and in order."

The Church has a great challenge to be united in the basic teachings and practices of the Bible. If we cannot agree on everything, we should at least respect one another's positions especially if the issues don't have anything to do with our salvation and the essential doctrines of the Bible. We should study the Bible well enough to understand the application of symbols and tokens in the practising of our faith. Openness towards believers who have the revelation of spiritual things helps us to appropriate the depths of revelation for our spiritual benefit.

Those who are sceptical about the anointing oil and tokens due to ignorance, miss their opportunities to be healed or blessed. Naaman, the commander of the armies of Benhadad II of Syria, nearly forfeited his healing because of his narrow mindedness about the operations of God. He knew about the token of the laying on of hands but not the dipping of his body into the River Jordan. Elisha the prophet asked him to do the latter. After much persuasion from his servants, he succumbed and was completely healed of his leprosy.

So Naaman came with his horses and with his chariot, and stood at the door of the house of Elisha.

And Elisha sent a messenger unto him, saying, Go and wash in Jordan seven times, and thy flesh shall come again to thee, and thou shalt be clean.

But Naaman was wroth, and went away, and said, Behold, I thought, He will surely come out to me, and stand, and call on the name of the LORD his God, and strike his hand over the place, and recover the leper.

Are not Abana and Pharpar, rivers of Damascus, better than all the waters of Israel? may I not wash in them, and be clean? So he turned and went away in a rage.

And his servants came near, and spake unto him, and said, My father, if the prophet had bid thee do some great thing, wouldest thou not have done it? how much rather then, when he saith to thee, Wash, and be clean?

Then went he down, and dipped himself seven times in Jordan, according to the saying of the man of God: and his flesh came again like unto the flesh of a little child, and he was clean.

2 Kings 5:9-14

Preachers and teachers use Naaman's story to teach about salvation and obedience. They claim that they believe God healed Naaman miraculously. The big question arises as to how many preachers today would direct a sick person to go and wash in water to be healed or receive the impartation of the Spirit. I am afraid that most preachers don't really believe most of the things they refer to in the Bible. It is pretence to believe in something that is written in the Bible but refuse to believe it can happen today. Anointing someone with oil is not as offensive as dipping him or her in a river.

If we claim to believe in anything that is written in the Bible but do not do it and cannot accept its practice today, we are living in deception.

The Bible does not make it compulsory for one to use the anointing oil before one is healed or receives the impartation of the Spirit. In the same way, the Bible does not forbid anyone who prefers to believe God for the impartation of the Spirit through the use of the anointing oil from doing so.

I find it difficult to understand those who argue that we should not use anointing oil for even healing because it is not scriptural, nonetheless they use medicines and see doctors though the Bible does not command them to do so. Why would one patronise medications and condemn the use of the anointing oil? Why would someone believe in psychological therapy and despise the power of the laying on of hands and anointing with oil? A good number of those who condemn the use of symbols and tokens can afford the best medical attention from doctors. They should remember that most believers can only rely on the supernatural means God makes available for their blessing.

You can be made whole if you discover the operational key to your breakthrough and are humble enough to obey the voice of God.

There is a section of preachers who teach that the anointing oil should be used for only healing. They don't believe that the anointing oil serves the purpose of the impartation of the anointing as prescribed in the Old Testament. As we saw earlier, James 5:14 shows that like prayer, the name of Jesus and the elders of the church, the anointing oil serves other purposes for the edification of the Church. If we walk in the Word and obedience, the anointing can be of great benefit to believers.

If we maintain proper ethics and decorum the use of the anointing oil can bring great benefits to the Body of Christ. Many questions arise from the use of the anointing oil. One of the most frequently asked questions is whether it is biblical to anoint everyone in a service of many hundreds or thousands of people. The answer to this question is "yes!" It is possible for everybody in a service to be filled with the Spirit.

The Spirit of God fell on all the seventy people Moses selected in the wilderness. The Spirit even fell on Eldad and Medad who were not at the Tabernacle. If all the seventy received the Spirit including those who were not at the Tabernacle, it is easier for God to put His Spirit on everyone in a building.

And Moses went out, and told the people the words of the LORD, and gathered the seventy men of the elders of the people, and set them round about the tabernacle.

And the LORD came down in a cloud, and spake unto him, and took of the spirit that was upon him, and gave it unto the seventy elders: and it came to pass, that, when the spirit rested upon them, they prophesied, and did not cease.

But there remained two of the men in the camp, the name of the one was Eldad, and the name of the other Medad: and the spirit rested upon them; and they were of them that were

written, but went not out unto the tabernacle:
and they prophesied in the camp.

Numbers 11:24-26

On the day of Pentecost, all the one hundred and twenty people in the Upper Room were filled with the Holy Ghost. Everybody in the Upper Room was filled with the Holy Ghost including Thomas who is noted for his ability to doubt and Peter who had denied Christ. There might have been people in the Upper Room who were worse than Thomas and Peter but were filled with the Holy Ghost. It is possible for God to fill everybody in a huge hall with the Holy Ghost.

And when the day of Pentecost was fully come,
they were all with one accord in one place.

And suddenly there came a sound from
heaven as of a rushing mighty wind, and it
filled all the house where they were sitting.

And there appeared unto them cloven
tongues like as of fire, and it sat upon each of
them.

And they were all filled with the Holy Ghost,
and began to speak with other tongues, as the
Spirit gave them utterance.

Acts 2:1-4

After the release of Peter and John by Caiaphas and the council, the disciples who gathered to pray

39

were all filled with the Holy Ghost. Some of the disciples might have been fearful and doubtful as a result of the persecution of the time. In spite of this, they were all filled with the Holy Ghost. Faith is a prerequisite for spiritual blessing but God's mercy can make Him bless us in spite of our fears and doubt.

And being let go, they went to their own company, and reported all that the chief priests and elders had said unto them.

And when they heard that, they lifted up their voice to God with one accord, and said, Lord, thou art God, which hast made heaven, and earth, and the sea, and all that in them is:

And when they had prayed, the place was shaken where they were assembled together; and they were all filled with the Holy Ghost, and they spake the word of God with boldness.

Acts 4:23-24, 31

Though God is able to fill everybody with the Holy Ghost it is our responsibility to select the right candidates for the impartation. Peter refused to lay his hands on Simon the Sorcerer. The Bible says we should lay hands on no man suddenly. It is presumptuous to go about laying hands on everybody. Those who lay hands on unrepentant sinners and believers who live in sin become partakers of their sins.

Lay hands suddenly on no man, neither be partaker of other men's sins: keep thyself pure.
1 Timothy 5:22

There is the risk of imparting the anointing to the wrong candidates and receiving demonic influences from sinful people. In spite of the risk, we can lay hands on everybody based on the instructions we give to people who step forward to be anointed. It is similar to what we do during a communion service. We instruct those who come to the table to examine themselves and pray before they step forward to take the communion. Specific instruction prevents the wrong people from going forward to be anointed.

Wherefore whosoever shall eat this bread, and drink this cup of the Lord, unworthily, shall be guilty of the body and blood of the Lord.

But let a man examine himself, and so let him eat of that bread, and drink of that cup.

For he that eateth and drinketh unworthily, eateth and drinketh damnation to himself, not discerning the Lord's body.

For this cause many are weak and sickly among you, and many sleep.

For if we would judge ourselves, we should not be judged.
1 Corinthians 11:27-31

Instead of condemning the act of laying hands on everybody and anointing them in a service, it is better to teach the Body of Christ to do things with decorum. Orderliness and self-examination are healthy for effective impartation of the Spirit. As much as it is the responsibility of a minister to know those he or she should anoint, it is equally the responsibility of believers to ensure that they don't rush into God's presence without caution.

I have the spiritual favour from God to lay hands on people and anoint them with oil almost on a weekly basis. In a good number of services each month I lay hands on thousands of people and anoint them with oil in various services. During anointing services in large meetings I lay hands on five to eight thousand people alone without collapsing from exhaustion. In such meetings, I ensure that the atmosphere is orderly and spiritual. Ushers and singers play major roles in ensuring that the presence of God is in the meeting and the people are organised to receive the anointing without commotion. No matter how chaotic a meeting becomes in terms of congregants falling under the power and running about, I instruct ushers to take charge of the meeting. The ushers at the Desert Pastures, Fountain Gate Chapel, where I serve as Senior Pastor are well-trained ushers who can minister alongside me for over two hours without me uttering a word. I have trained them to interpret signs with my hands, eyes, lips and head.

We must not discard the ministry of anointing believers with oil because of ignorance on the subject and its abuse by some ministers. It is ignorance to contend that we must intellectually understand the use of anointing oil before we use it. After all, we appropriate the power of the name and blood of Jesus without natural understanding. Believers abuse the blood of Jesus by sprinkling it on their human enemies in prayer, but that does not stop us from believing in its efficacy. We don't have to throw away the baby with the bath water.

The anointing oil represents the spiritual anointing of the Holy Ghost. Applying the anointing oil on believers releases the power of God on them in ways that are similar to the functions of physical oil in day-to-day life. When we pray over oil and dedicate it to God, it ceases to be a mere physical thing and assumes a spiritual purpose. The sanctified oil acquires sacramental value. A sacrament is when something that is physical is used to convey spiritual grace. The oil is nothing without prayer and dedication but when it is committed to God it carries supernatural power. Once oil is dedicated to God it becomes the holy anointing oil. It does not have to contain spices to release the power of God. Applying it in the name of Jesus gives it the power of efficacy since the spices in the anointing oil of the Tabernacle represented the holy and powerful nature of Christ. In the remaining chapters of this book we shall look at the common uses of olive oil, beginning from its medicinal purposes. These uses of oil in the natural realm have their corresponding uses in the spiritual realm. What physical oil does to your body and domestic life, the anointing of the Holy Ghost does in your spiritual life.

CHAPTER 4

OIL FOR HEALING

In a service in which I was ministering in December 1991, at a point I was in the Spirit and saw droplets of oil all over the building among the congregation. It was a captivating scene. I asked the Lord to show me the meaning of what I saw and He said the hearts of His people and their emotions were being healed. Immediately, I told the congregation what the Lord had told me. Almost spontaneously, people began to weep in joy and many were set free from hurt and depression. The Holy Ghost as oil brings healing to the spirit, the soul and the body.

Olive oil has been used for centuries to treat medical conditions. In modern times, it is still very useful in compounding antibacterial and antifungal ointments. The scientific explanation for the healing properties of olive oil is that it is high in antioxidants and contains Vitamin K, which makes it useful in the treatment of skin tumours and it is believed to help in the prevention of skin cancer. It is used to remove earwax and cure earaches. Other health benefits of olive oil are the treatment of diabetes, high blood cholesterol, and complications due to old age. Regular intake of olive of oil enhances weight loss.

In Bible times, shepherds used oil on the bruises and wounds of sheep though probably without any scientific knowledge. The Lord is our Shepherd who anoints our heads with oil for healing and refreshing. When God anoints our heads with oil, healing flows to the rest of our bodies and lives.

The LORD is my shepherd; I shall not want.

He maketh me to lie down in green pastures: he leadeth me beside the still waters.

He restoreth my soul: he leadeth me in the paths of righteousness for his name's sake.

Yea, though I walk through the valley of the shadow of death, I will fear no evil: for thou art with me; thy rod and thy staff they comfort me.

Thou preparest a table before me in the presence of mine enemies: thou anointest my head with oil; my cup runneth over.

Surely goodness and mercy shall follow me all the days of my life: and I will dwell in the house of the LORD for ever.

Psalm 23:1-6

The parable of the Good Samaritan depicts the healing power of oil. In this parable, the Good Samaritan applied oil to the wounds of a traveller who was attacked by thieves on the way from Jerusalem to Jericho.

And Jesus answering said, A certain man went down from Jerusalem to Jericho, and fell among thieves, which stripped him of his raiment, and wounded him, and departed, leaving him half dead.

And by chance there came down a certain priest that way: and when he saw him, he passed by on the other side.

And likewise a Levite, when he was at the place, came and looked on him, and passed by on the other side.

But a certain Samaritan, as he journeyed, came where he was: and when he saw him, he had compassion on him,

And went to him, and bound up his wounds, pouring in oil and wine, and set him on his own beast, and brought him to an inn, and took care of him.

Luke 10:30-34

The Good Samaritan poured wine and oil on the traveller's wounds. Wine contains ethyl alcohol and methyl alcohol, which are disinfectants. Olive oil has emollient properties and acts as a moisturiser and disinfectant.

Jesus' disciples anointed the sick with oil and healed them. Oil is a symbol of the Holy Ghost and when it is used, the Holy Ghost works in the lives of the sick in ways that are similar to the effects of oil in the physical realm. The Holy Ghost heals all manner of diseases just as the olive oil cures many diseases. The power of oil to heal does not come from the oil but from the Holy Ghost. The oil simply reminds us about the fact that the Holy Ghost is the source of healing.

And they cast out many devils, and anointed with oil many that were sick, and healed them.
Mark 6:13

Do not get nervous about the use of oil to anoint the sick because fake people have abused its use by making a fetish out of it and creating an oil-dependency syndrome. Many things have been abused in the lives of other people but that has not stopped us from patronising them. Money, husbands, wives, computers and vehicles are abused but we still patronise them.

There is no power in oil and oil cannot be holy. It is called "holy oil" because it is dedicated to the LORD and is used for purposes of sanctification and consecration (Psalm 89:20). We must desist from abusing the use of the anointing oil because it ceases to be ordinary oil when it is dedicated to God. God works with it to perform His counsel.

Prayer and faith must accompany the use of oil to make it efficacious. The power lies in the name of Jesus and the power of the Holy Ghost when the oil is in use. The Apostle James directed that the sick should be prayed for and anointed with oil for their healing.

> *Is any sick among you? let him call for the elders of the church; and let them pray over him, anointing him with oil in the name of the Lord:*
> *And the prayer of faith shall save the sick, and the Lord shall raise him up; and if he have committed sins, they shall be forgiven him.*
> *James 5:14-15*

The prayer of faith in the name of the Lord heals the sick. The admonition that the elders be called indicates that oil in the hands of unbelieving fellows pretending to heal the sick will do no good. Oil in the hands of immature believers leads to confusion. Holy, wise and disciplined elders of the Church must apply it. While it is scriptural to acknowledge the roles of prayer and the elders in healing, we cannot discount the role the anointing oil plays. Let us appropriate the spiritual power behind the symbol, and avoid the idolatry of its form.

The evidence of healing by using anointing oil is too common among believers to deny its effect. I have personally witnessed God heal many people through prayer coupled with the application of anointing oil. One evening, I went to church in Bolgatanga and spoke on healing through prayer and anointing with oil. After a short teaching, I asked members who were sick to sit on chairs in front of the church and the pastors and leaders of the church prayed for them and anointed them with oil. Immediately after the prayer, many of those who were prayed for gave testimonies of healing. A lady told me after about five months that she had been having heart palpitations for years, but after the prayer she had not experienced any.

A few years ago, I was ministering in the City Church of God in Kumasi, Ghana and a spectacular miracle happened. I finished teaching and praying for people and as I was receiving the offering a woman screamed from the congregation that her daughter who was about twenty years old had died beside her. There was instant pandemonium in the church but I was moved by the Holy Ghost to say "people don't die in church." There was no doctor there to confirm she was dead but if a girl's mother says she is dead you can't take that for granted. When the Shunammite woman's son died there was no doctor to confirm his death but we believe a miracle of raising the dead took place.

After uttering the profound statement "people don't die in church", I stepped forward to where the woman and her daughter were sitting and found the latter stretched out and stiff on the pew with her eyes shut and not blinking. She did not seem to be breathing. Her mother ran out of the church auditorium, knelt down on the ground and lifted up her hands to God, crying that He should save her daughter. I instructed the ushers to carry the unconscious or dead girl into a side room and I called the Bishop of the church and some pastors to come in and help me pray for her. I poured oil on her head, anointed her face and we prayed for her.

After praying for about five minutes I left them in the room and went back to the auditorium to continue the meeting. I did that to prevent the devil from taking over the atmosphere. While the congregation was singing I went back to the room and found the pastors and leaders still praying for the young lady. I stood over her and shouted the name of Jesus and commanded her to live. She was immediately revived and opened her eyes and we all went back to the auditorium, the congregation rejoicing with us.

I cannot attribute this miracle only to the use of

anointing oil but it played a part. Using it was part of the process of releasing the faith that made the miracle possible. The anointing oil is a powerful tool that facilitates the release of the supernatural power of God in healing and deliverance. The anointing oil is effective because it represents the Holy Ghost. We must embrace the total counsel of God in order to receive the grace He makes available to the Church.

When people are anointed with oil they are healed because of their faith in the person of the Holy Ghost. The anointing purifies us, makes us acceptable, beautifies us, makes us wholesome and creates harmony among us. Anointing believers with oil imparts to them the power of the Holy Ghost. The anointing oil as a symbol of the Holy Ghost reminds us of God's holiness and His power to cleanse believers by the power of the Holy Ghost. Faith and prayer release the power of the Holy Ghost when the oil is applied. In the next chapter we shall consider the anointing of the Holy Ghost as a cleansing factor.

CHAPTER 5

OIL FOR CLEANSING

It is a known fact that oil dissolves oil. Hence olive oil and castor oil are used as facial cleansers and moisturisers. Olive oil is used for cleansing and purification of the skin from dirt in places like Morocco. It leaves behind a refreshing and pleasant feeling. Under dry weather conditions, shepherds anoint sheep's heads with oil and this leaves a refreshing feeling on them. The Psalmist refers to the anointing of sheep's heads with oil by saying the LORD anoints his head with oil.

> *Thou preparest a table before me in the presence of mine enemies: thou anointest my head with oil; my cup runneth over.*
>
> *Psalm 23:5*

In our day as well as in Bible times, oil is employed in the manufacturing of soap, which has a powerful cleansing effect. A world without soap would be a dirty place. Jeremiah compared the cleansing power of the Holy Ghost with that of soap, which is a product of oil.

For though thou wash thee with nitre, and take thee much soap, yet thine iniquity is marked before me, saith the Lord GOD.

Jeremiah 2:22

The above verse mentions two cleansing agents namely nitre and soap. Nitre (potassium nitrate), which is also called saltpetre, is used in the treatment of poisoning. Potassium compounds referred to as potash are mixed with oil to form soap, which is a cleansing agent. Oil is an important component of soap and so the mention of soap in the above verse implies the function of oil.

The Holy Ghost and the anointing cleanse believers in several ways. He convicts believers of sin and leads them to repentance and the repentance brings cleansing. The Psalmist pleaded with God to create in him a clean heart and not to take the Holy Ghost from him. The presence of the Holy Ghost removes sin from the believer's life.

Create in me a clean heart, O God; and renew a right spirit within me.

Cast me not away from thy presence; and take not thy holy spirit from me.

Psalm 51:10-11

Constant sinning leads to bondage as people get enslaved by habits they find impossible to break. There are bondages the human will cannot break and it takes the anointing to break them.

And it shall come to pass in that day, that his burden shall be taken away from off thy shoulder, and his yoke from off thy neck, and the yoke shall be destroyed because of the anointing.

Isaiah 10:27

Sin is caused by demons, which lie to people, deceive them and lead them into disobedience. Demons build strongholds in the mind and fill people with anger, hatred and lust. Casting out demons cleanses those who are filled with them. Jesus cast out devils by the Spirit of God thereby cleansing those He ministered to.

But if I cast out devils by the Spirit of God, then the kingdom of God is come unto you.

Matthew 12:28

Casting out devils produces lasting results only when the people who have the devils cast out of them are filled with the Spirit of God. If the person remains empty, the devils that are cast out of him or her, return with more wicked ones.

When the unclean spirit is gone out of a man, he walketh through dry places, seeking rest; and finding none, he saith, I will return unto my house whence I came out.

And when he cometh, he findeth it swept and garnished.

Then goeth he, and taketh to him seven other spirits more wicked than himself; and they enter in, and dwell there: and the last state of that man is worse than the first.

Luke 11:24-26

The Holy Ghost produces the fruit of the Spirit in believers and makes them pure in spirit. When believers are saturated with the fruit of the Spirit, it prevents demons from re-entering them.

But the fruit of the Spirit is love, joy, peace, longsuffering, gentleness, goodness, faith,

Meekness, temperance: against such there is no law.

Galatians 5:22-23

The combined fruit of love, joy, peace, longsuffering, gentleness, goodness, faith, meekness and temperance preserve the heart from the corruption of sin and evil. If we confess our sins and repent of them, the Holy Ghost works in us to produce God's righteousness. The oil of the Holy Ghost does not remove sins that are not confessed.

The Holy Ghost does not condone wilful indulgence in carnality. The forgiving and cleansing of sins produce joy and gladness. Joy is part of the fruit of the Spirit. It is a characteristic thing to see the outbreak of joy and gladness when the Holy Ghost moves among believers.

Jesus loved righteousness and God anointed Him with the oil of gladness. Joy empowers the believer to live victoriously and to praise God. The Holy Ghost works in us to be righteous in order to uncap the well of joy in us.

Thou hast loved righteousness, and hated iniquity; therefore God, even thy God, hath anointed thee with the oil of gladness above thy fellows.

Hebrews 1:9

The anointing is the oil of gladness. God does not leave us condemned and tormented after we have confessed our sins and repented of them. A believer who has perpetual guilt has either not confessed his sins or has refused to repent. The Psalmist says the creation of a new heart and the joy of salvation are connected.

Create in me a clean heart, O God; and renew a right spirit within me.
    Cast me not away from thy presence; and take not thy holy spirit from me.

Restore unto me the joy of thy salvation; and uphold me with thy free spirit.

Psalm 51:10-12

Righteousness produces peace and joy in the Holy Ghost. It is vain to pray for peace and joy when you are not righteous. The Holy Ghost cleanses us from the corruption of sin and gives us peace and joy.

For the kingdom of God is not meat and drink; but righteousness, and peace, and joy in the Holy Ghost.

Romans 14:17

The reason for which God cleanses us from sin is to give us peace and joy. The benefits of righteousness go beyond having peace and joy. They include the favour of acceptance and admission into God's presence. By using the anointing oil we activate our faith in the power of the Holy Ghost to break the yoke of sin and give us favour to go into God's presence. We shall consider the favour the Holy Ghost gives us in the next chapter.

CHAPTER 6

OIL FOR FAVOUR

Oil is used to express courtesy towards guests. It refreshes the body and makes them attractive. There are two kinds of anointing when it comes to guests. In the first, the oil is applied to the person to give him or her favour to come into the presence of another person. The second kind of anointing is for staying in God's presence and functioning there.

A typical illustration of how the anointing brings someone into God's presence is the anointing of Esther with the oil of myrrh and other fragrances before she came into the king's presence.

Now when every maid's turn was come to go in to king Ahasuerus, after that she had been twelve months, according to the manner of the women, (for so were the days of their purifications accomplished, to wit, six months with oil of myrrh, and six months with sweet odours, and with other things for the purifying of the women;)

Then thus came every maiden unto the king; whatsoever she desired was given her to go with her out of the house of the women unto the king's house.

In the evening she went, and on the morrow she returned into the second house of the women, to the custody of Shaashgaz, the king's chamberlain, which kept the concubines: she came in unto the king no more, except the king delighted in her, and that she were called by name.

Now when the turn of Esther, the daughter of Abihail the uncle of Mordecai, who had taken her for his daughter, was come to go in unto the king, she required nothing but what Hegai the king's chamberlain, the keeper of the women, appointed. And Esther obtained favour in the sight of all them that looked upon her.

So Esther was taken unto king Ahasuerus into his house royal in the tenth month, which is the month Tebeth, in the seventh year of his reign.

And the king loved Esther above all the women, and she obtained grace and favour in *his sight more than all the virgins; so that he set the royal crown upon her head, and made her queen instead of Vashti.*

Then the king made a great feast unto all his princes and his servants, even Esther's feast; and he made a release to the provinces, and gave gifts, according to the state of the king.

Esther 2:12-18

Esther did not indiscriminately apply substances to her body like the other ladies who went into the king's presence. They depended on their own wisdom and selected many items, which were not recommended by Hegai the king's Eunuch in charge of the women. Esther on the other hand used only what Hegai prescribed for her.

We can only come into God's presence through the anointing of the Holy Ghost. No flesh can glory in His presence. We cannot go into God's presence with our human ideas and strength. Many people try to impress God by resorting to man-made things. We don't need sophistication to please God. The anointing is pure and simple and it is all we need.

The oil of myrrh was one of the fragrances Esther used before she went into the king's presence. It was a gum resin extracted from the plant **Commiphora Myrrha**, which grows in dry and stony areas. The tree bark is wounded into the sapwood to bleed the resin. Myrrh was an ingredient in the holy anointing oil of the Tabernacle. It was used for incense and perfumes. Myrrh as a stimulant contains essential oils that stimulate blood circulation, digestion, nerve function and excretion. It also acts as a pulmonary stimulant. Myrrh was used against fungal infections and as an antiseptic, it was used for embalming and for repelling insects in Ancient Egypt. It is an anti-inflammatory agent and a powerful antioxidant. Modern scientists are exploring avenues to use it in the treatment of cancers and tumours. Myrrh is effective in skin care – it promotes healthy skin, heals chapped skin and is an anti-aging substance.

As a perfume, the myrrh gave Esther an agreeable smell that attracted the king. This is similar to what the anointing of the Holy Ghost does in our lives – it gives us the fragrance of holiness, wisdom, grace, peace, joy and faith when we come before God. The oil of myrrh was used for embalming and that suggests its ability to slow down the process of decay. It prevented Esther from producing unwanted odour. The anointing keeps us from getting corrupted by sin and from being destroyed by demons and diseases. The oil of myrrh "stimulated" Esther when she entered the king's presence. She was elegant, confident, intelligent and creative. The anointing of the Holy Ghost produces similar effects in us.

The fact that a tree is bled to release the oil of myrrh suggests that suffering for Christ's sake generates the anointing in you. If you are broken through sacrifice and obedience, the anointing in you flows out. *Commiphora Myrrha* grows in dry and stony places. This must encourage you to have faith that if God plants you in "a dry place" your mission will still be fulfilled. Your physical location cannot prevent the anointing from flowing through your life.

Esther received the anointing to come into the king's presence. There is another kind of anointing one receives after one enters God's presence. The woman with the alabaster box of ointment anointed Jesus' feet with this kind of anointing when He went to Simon the Pharisee's house. The anointing of a guest with oil by his or her host was a great act of courtesy. It was an act of graciousness and expression of great fondness. Jesus queried Simon, into whose house He went, when he failed to anoint His head and feet with oil.

And he turned to the woman, and said unto Simon, Seest thou this woman? I entered into thine house, thou gavest me no water for my feet: but she hath washed my feet with tears, and wiped them with the hairs of her head.

Thou gavest me no kiss: but this woman

since the time I came in hath not ceased to kiss my feet.

My head with oil thou didst not anoint: but this woman hath anointed my feet with ointment.

Luke 7:44-46

The Pharisee did not anoint Jesus' head with oil but the sinful woman anointed His feet with ointment. The Greek word for "oil" in the above verse is **elaion**, which is mere oil base such as olive oil. This oil was ordinary and cheap though it had a favourable smell. The Pharisee did not even use it for Jesus' head. He received Jesus into his house but was so religiously prejudiced that he could not maximise the moment. His religious spirit prevented him from receiving the blessing of having Jesus in his house.

The woman, on the other hand, anointed Jesus' feet with ointment. The Greek word for "ointment" is **myron**. The **myron** is perfumed oil which is used for the head and other parts of the body that are regarded as noble. The woman with the alabaster box of ointment anointed His feet, which are supposedly His less noble parts with the ointment. The oil was expensive but the woman deemed it necessary to anoint Jesus with it.

Just as oil imparts beauty and fragrance to the

human body, the anointing of the Holy Ghost imparts glory and majesty to our spirits and souls. By giving us the Holy Ghost, God extends a great act of courtesy and welcome towards us, as He ushers us into the Kingdom of God. This gives us confidence in His presence.

There are two main stages of activity of the Holy Ghost in the believer's life. The first stage is His activity of convicting him or her of sin and regenerating him or her. This stage gives one the favour to be admitted into God's presence like Esther was received into the king's presence. The second stage is the empowering of the believer to bear fruit and to work the works of God. At this point the person is already ushered into God's presence and receives the anointing for service. It is comparable with how Jesus was received into Simon's house and the woman anointed His feet with oil. Two types of favour are portrayed in these two scenarios.

Perfumed or spiced oil has great cosmetic value. It produces a fragrance and causes the face to glow and softens the skin. In Bible days, men mostly used oil whereas women used ointments. Spiritually, the oil of the Holy Ghost makes our faces shine. The anointing makes us stand out.

And wine that maketh glad the heart of man,

and oil to make his face to shine, and bread which strengtheneth man's heart.

Psalm 104:15

The above verse mentions three things that empower and embolden a person– wine, oil and bread. These three things have spiritual significance. Wine and oil are symbols of the Holy Ghost and bread is a symbol of the Word of God. The anointing makes the heart glad and this gladness flashes on the outside and causes the face to shine. The Word of God gives strength to a man's spirit to maintain and increase the anointing on his life.

A testimony from one of my meetings in Accra, Ghana, in 2011 demonstrates the power of the anointing to beautify and give favour to a person. In this service I finished preaching and the Spirit moved me to lay hands on people and anoint them with oil. At a certain point I called a woman forward who looked absent-minded, sad and completely dejected. Her countenance had no expression whatsoever. I anointed her with oil and laid my hands on her. She fell under the power gently and lay on the floor for about fifteen minutes. The meeting closed and we all went home. The next day I was in the office after another night's meeting when a sister I knew walked in with the woman I had ministered to the previous night. She looked refreshed and beautiful with broad smiles radiating from her face.

The woman I knew narrated the lady's story to me. She had two children and one of them had just died under strange circumstances. The incident completely devastated her and she lost her peace. She was dying within. They explained that after the ministration she got up from the floor feeling weak like someone who had had a thorough massage. She went home and slept under the influence of the anointing and when she got up the next morning she was completely refreshed. She received the peace and joy of the Holy Ghost and her spirit was revived. Anointing people who are discouraged or devastated with oil revives them. The Holy Ghost comes upon them and gives them peace and joy. The Holy Ghost makes the heart glad and causes the face to shine.

The anointing oil stirs up our faith in the power of the Holy Ghost. Many believers who are anointed with oil get soaked with oil and fall under that power in vain because they don't have the revelation of the benefits of the anointing oil. They fail to connect the anointing oil with the presence of the person of the Holy Ghost.

The Bible reveals other purposes of the anointing in the believer's life like the tempering of sacrifices with oil. Some items that were used for sacrifices in the Tabernacle were mingled with oil to burn them to the LORD. Oil was poured on sacrifices to signify that they were holy onto the LORD. The use of anointing oil on believers has similar implications as the use of the oil on sacrifices. In the next chapter we shall consider the powerful effect of the anointing oil on the believer as a living sacrifice to God.

CHAPTER **7**

OIL FOR SACRIFICES

S pritually, some sacrifices in the Old Testament were seasoned with oil. One of such offerings was the grain or meal offering of the firstfruits, which was made at the harvest time. This offering was a type of Jesus offering Himself as a sacrifice without blemish to the Father. The detailed description of the meal offering provides interesting revelations about the offering of Christ including the tempering of the offering with oil.

And if thou offer a meat offering of thy firstfruits unto the LORD, thou shalt offer for the meat offering of thy firstfruits green ears of corn dried by the fire, even corn beaten out of full ears.

And thou shalt put oil upon it, and lay frankincense thereon: it is a meat offering.

And the priest shall burn the memorial of it,

part of the beaten corn thereof, and part of the
oil thereof, with all the frankincense thereof: it
is an offering made by fire unto the LORD.
Leviticus 2:14-16

The grain offering consisted of crushed heads of new grain mixed with oil and incense that was burnt in the fire. In the typology of the grain offering, the fine flour shows the perfect humanity and character of Christ. The oil is a type of the anointing of the Holy Ghost on Christ as He lived, ministered and offered Himself as a sacrifice on earth. The incense (frankincense) represented His affable and agreeable personality. Yeast was absent from the grain offering to signify Christ's sinless nature.

Jesus Christ referred to Himself as the grain of wheat that would be buried in the earth and bear much fruit. By this He meant His death and resurrection.

Verily, verily, I say unto you, Except a corn of
wheat fall into the ground and die, it abideth
alone: but if it die, it bringeth forth much fruit.
John 12:24

Jesus Christ offered His body as a sacrifice through His holy living, complete dedication to the Father and ultimately through His death on the Cross of Calvary.

Wherefore when he cometh into the world, he saith, Sacrifice and offering thou wouldest not, but a body hast thou prepared me:

In burnt offerings and sacrifices for sin thou hast had no pleasure.

Hebrews 10:5-6

We saw earlier that God accepted the grain offering only when it was tempered with oil and incense. The oil represented the Holy Ghost. In the same manner Christ offered Himself as a spotless sacrifice through the power of the eternal Spirit of God – the anointing of the Holy Ghost.

How much more shall the blood of Christ, who through the eternal Spirit offered himself without spot to God, purge your conscience from dead works to serve the living God?

Hebrews 9:14

Many believers don't know that the only way Jesus could have had a successful ministry was through the power of the Holy Ghost. He was baptised in the Holy Ghost for ministry. He also offered Himself in the medium of the Spirit just as the grain offering was mixed with oil. The Holy Ghost gave Jesus His sinless and perfect nature. He operated in Christ to know the will of God and pray according to that will. The Holy Ghost empowered Jesus to die on the Cross. He had the power to endure the pain of

71

crucifixion without resisting God's will. The Spirit of God raised Jesus from the dead.

> *And if Christ be in you, the body is dead because of sin; but the Spirit is life because of righteousness.*
>
> *But if the Spirit of him that raised up Jesus from the dead dwell in you, he that raised up Christ from the dead shall also quicken your mortal bodies by his Spirit that dwelleth in you.*
>
> *Romans 8:10-11*

Jesus Christ offered Himself as a sacrifice and those who believe in Him have to follow His example. Believers are to present their bodies as living sacrifices unto God like the grain offering was presented. Bodies that are offered to God must be living sacrifices that are holy and acceptable.

> *I beseech you therefore, brethren, by the mercies of God, that ye present your bodies a living sacrifice, holy, acceptable unto God, which is your reasonable service.*
>
> *Romans 12:1*

The phrase "living sacrifice" refers to a sacrifice that is wholesome and pleasing to God. Such sacrifices must be physically alive and without any deformity. They have to meet specified standards. With reference to human beings, sacrifices presented to God must be spiritually wholesome. Spiritually wholesome people are holy, they are obedient to God, they commune with God and they are filled with the Holy Ghost. Apart from being spiritually wholesome, human beings who present themselves as living sacrifices must do so when they are physically and emotionally healthy. Some people refuse to consecrate themselves to God until they are sick, too old or emotionally wrecked. God prefers living sacrifices to dead ones.

God accepts sacrifices that are well pleasing unto Him. He does not accept just anything. The Apostle Paul told the Philippians that their sweet smelling gifts were acceptable and well pleasing to God.

But I have all, and abound: I am full, having received of Epaphroditus the things which were sent from you, an odour of a sweet smell, a sacrifice acceptable, wellpleasing to God.

Philippians 4:18

Paul received the gifts of the Philippians and used them but the sweet smell of the sacrifices went up to God. This is similar to the sacrifices in the Tabernacle or Temple. The priests ate the meat or meal, the ashes remained on the altar but the smoke (the smell) rose up to God. When we bring our offerings to church today, the Church uses the offerings but the smell of our energy and lives go up to God.

The anointing makes a sacrifice alive. It imparts life to the sacrifice just as perfumed oil imparts a sweet fragrance to a grain offering. Oil on an offering makes it acceptable to God. Anointing people with oil consecrates them to God. The awareness of the presence of the Holy Ghost produces a holy disposition in believers and this makes them acceptable unto God.

My ministry features many anointing services as earlier mentioned where I anoint hundreds and sometimes thousands of believers with the anointing oil and lay hands on them. The reasons for the anointing services are mainly to consecrate people for the work of the ministry, to stir up the gifts of the Holy Ghost, to heal the sick and to break demonic oppressions. I have witnessed God do amazing things in people's lives as a result of these services. People approach the anointing services with reverence and faith. They come in their thousands ready to receive from God. Testimonies of healing and deliverance are reported. Believers receive unction for prayer and ministry. Others are empowered to give money and material things for the work of the ministry. Tears run down the cheeks of those who are filled with joy and moved to repentance. Singing and dancing in the Spirit characterise these meetings. Shouts of victory and holy prostrations combine to produce refreshing atmospheres.

In one of such meetings, I anointed a lady and laid hands on her. As I ministered to her the Holy Ghost came upon her and she fell under the power away from me. She finally lay prostrate at the pulpit and the Lord told me she was dedicated to Him for the ministry and would marry a pastor. True to the prophecy she married a pastor later on and they are in the ministry together. This lady was consecrated to the Lord by being anointed with oil like the grain offering, which was burnt to the Lord.

The anointing oil reminds us about the work of the Holy Ghost. It portrays what the Holy Ghost does in the spiritual realm, in the physical realm. To attack the use of oil and the laying on of hands is to quench the Spirit. Another effect of oil in the Bible is to provide light in the Tabernacle. Oil was put in the lamps to act as fuel. The anointing of the Holy Ghost makes us shine like lights. It generates supernatural zeal in us to accomplish God's purposes. In the next chapter, we shall consider the purpose of the anointing oil as fuel.

CHAPTER 8

OIL FOR FUEL

God instructed Moses to command the children of Israel to bring pure olive oil for the lamps of the Tabernacle to provide light. God is light and His dwelling place had to have light continuously. It is interesting to note that God required the children of Israel to bring the oil for the lamps. He could have asked the priests to provide the oil but He asked the people to do so. The symbolism here is that it takes the body of believers to keep the anointing flowing and the light of Christ burning. It is wrong for believers to depend solely on the fivefold ministry for the anointing.

And thou shalt command the children of Israel, that they bring thee pure oil olive beaten for the light, to cause the lamp to burn always.

In the tabernacle of the congregation without the vail, which is before the testimony, Aaron and his sons shall order it from evening to morning before the LORD: it shall be a statute for ever unto their generations on the behalf of the children of Israel.

Exodus 27:20-21

The "pure oil olive beaten" referred to the "mother drop" that dropped out first when the olives were bruised in the mortar before they were put under the press or before the application of fire. This oil is comparable with the fresh anointing. It shows that the best anointing is the kind that flows out without too much human effort. The pure olive oil was fuel for the lamps in the Tabernacle.

In normal life in Bible times, oil served as fuel for lamps made of clay or brass. The Holy Ghost illuminates the hearts of men with revelation just as oil produces light in lamps. He enables believers to burn with love, truth, faith and zeal. Jesus underscored the importance of oil in the parable of the Ten Virgins. In this parable, the five wise virgins took extra oil in vessels besides the oil in their lamps to go and meet the bridegroom. Unlike the wise virgins, the foolish ones failed to take extra oil in separate vessels with their lamps.

Then shall the kingdom of heaven be likened unto ten virgins, which took their lamps, and went forth to meet the bridegroom.

And five of them were wise, and five were foolish.

They that were foolish took their lamps, and took no oil with them:

But the wise took oil in their vessels with their lamps.

While the bridegroom tarried, they all slumbered and slept.

And at midnight there was a cry made, Behold, the bridegroom cometh; go ye out to meet him.

Then all those virgins arose, and trimmed their lamps.

And the foolish said unto the wise, Give us of your oil; for our lamps are gone out.

But the wise answered, saying, Not so; lest there be not enough for us and you: but go ye rather to them that sell, and buy for yourselves.

And while they went to buy, the bridegroom came; and they that were ready went in with him to the marriage: and the door was shut.

Afterward came also the other virgins, saying, Lord, Lord, open to us.

But he answered and said, Verily I say unto you, I know you not.

Watch therefore, for ye know neither the day nor the hour wherein the Son of man cometh.

Matthew 25:1-13

The bridegroom's delay precipitated a crisis – a shortage of oil in the ten virgins' lamps occurred. The level of preparedness of the wise and foolish virgins was laid bare. The wise virgins had enough oil to last the entire period but the foolish ones did not. All the ten virgins possessed the skill of trimming their lamps but only the wise ones with the extra oil received the bridegroom. The anointing makes the difference in our activities. We don't win the battles of life through our skills, physical strength and wisdom alone.

Then he answered and spake unto me, saying, This is the word of the LORD unto Zerubbabel, saying, Not by might, nor by power, but by my spirit, saith the LORD of hosts.

Zechariah 4:6

All the ten virgins rose up when they heard the announcement of the arrival of the bridegroom. They were all swift to awaken from their slumber but the foolish virgins were threatened with being plunged into darkness. They were awake and willing to meet the bridegroom but lacked oil in their lamps to do so.

I returned, and saw under the sun, that the race is not to the swift, nor the battle to the strong, neither yet bread to the wise, nor yet riches to men of understanding, nor yet favour to men of skill; but time and chance happeneth to them all.

Ecclesiastes 9:11

The Lord continuously fills us with the Holy Ghost so that we don't lack oil. We are filled with the Spirit as we receive the Word of God, as hands are laid on us, as we are anointed with oil and as we pray. If we increase in the anointing, the amount of light we generate becomes brighter and brighter. The psalmist said his horn would be exalted like the horn of a unicorn if God anointed him with fresh oil. By this, he meant God increased his strength by anointing him with oil.

But my horn shalt thou exalt like the horn of an unicorn: I shall be anointed with fresh oil.
Psalm 92:10

The word "fresh" in the above verse is the Hebrew word ***ra'anãn***, which means to be green and to flourish. No wonder the olive oil is greenish-yellow in colour. The psalmist knew that God anointed him with oil that kept him green like a tree and made him flourish.

Moses commanded the children of Israel to bring the olive oil to the Tabernacle constantly. If they stopped bringing it the lamps would go out. It is wrong to think that once you receive the Holy Ghost baptism you don't need to be filled with the Spirit. The infilling of the Spirit and increase of the anointing are on-going processes.

On the day of Pentecost one hundred and twenty disciples were filled with the Holy Ghost and spoke in other tongues as the Spirit gave them utterance.

And they were all filled with the Holy Ghost, and began to speak with other tongues, as the Spirit gave them utterance.

Acts 2:4

This was a phenomenal experience that shook the city of Jerusalem. One would think that if the disciples were filled with the Holy Ghost in that dramatic manner, they did not need any further infilling of the Holy Ghost. On the contrary, Peter, who was one of them was later filled with the Holy Ghost again when a challenging situation occurred. Challenges lead to infillings of the Holy Ghost.

And when they had set them in the midst, they asked, By what power, or by what name, have ye done this?

Then Peter, filled with the Holy Ghost, said unto them, Ye rulers of the people, and elders of Israel,

Acts 4:7-8

A group of the disciples of Christ were filled with the Holy Ghost when they gathered to pray. It is possible that some of them were in the Upper Room on the day of Pentecost and were already filled with the Holy Ghost. However, they were filled with the Holy Ghost again when they prayed.

And when they had prayed, the place was shaken where they were assembled together; and they were all filled with the Holy Ghost, and they spake the word of God with boldness.
Acts 4:31

The Apostle Paul admonished the Ephesians to be constantly filled with the Spirit. There is no limit to the number of times one can be filled with the Spirit. To be filled with the Spirit is to allow the Holy Ghost to have more of us. He is so infinite that we never have enough of Him.

And be not drunk with wine, wherein is excess; but be filled with the Spirit;
Speaking to yourselves in psalms and hymns and spiritual songs, singing and making melody in your heart to the Lord;
Ephesians 5:18-19

The Greek word for "be filled" is **plēroō** which means "to accomplish", "to fulfil", "to end", "to replenish" and "to finish". We have to keep being filled with the Spirit until we are "fully filled." The continuous infilling of the Holy Ghost gives us the power and zeal to accomplish God's purposes. The anointing acts as fuel to man's spirit to burn with zeal.

Not slothful in business; fervent in spirit; serving the Lord

Romans 12:11

The word "fervent" means "hot", "glowing" and "ardent". We must be hot in spirit and this can only be attained through the Spirit. The anointing energises and illuminates our spirits. We shine brighter and brighter in character and grow stronger and stronger in power.

The laying on of hands and anointing believers with oil multiplies workers in the Lord's service. In some parts of the Body of Christ, believers who practise the laying on of hands produce more ministers for the ministry than those who don't. They raise ministers faster than churches and ministries who depend on only the training of ministers in Bible schools. Bible schools are good for maintaining the doctrinal integrity and ethical sanity of the Church but the ministration of the Spirit should be encouraged in the Church. The apostolic and prophetic ministries experience great increase in manifestations of the Spirit and the number of ministers who are produced because of their dependence on the Holy Ghost.

Oil acts as fuel for lamps. Another common use of oil is its role as a lubricant. The Body of Christ consists of individuals and groups of believers who engage one another to propagate the Kingdom of

God. The anointing of the Holy Ghost ensures that believers operate smoothly with one another as they form the partnerships that are necessary for the work of the ministry. Without the anointing there will be constant misunderstanding, resistance and conflict among believers. In the final chapter of this book, we shall consider the purpose of the anointing as a lubricant in the functioning of the Body of Christ. The anointing is the agent of harmony in the Church.

CHAPTER 9

OIL FOR HARMONY

Oil is employed as a lubricant to prevent rust and also to minimise the friction between pieces of metal that rub together in machines. How can one maintain his spiritual fervour without rusting? How can brethren dwell together in unity in spite of different backgrounds and temperaments? How can we prevent disagreements amongst saints from having damaging effects on the Church of Jesus Christ?

When the anointing flows from the leader of the congregation, down to the associate minister and among the congregation, there is order in diversity. It is pleasant to see a group of believers operating in one anointing and having the same mind. Without the anointing the natural tendency is for believers to disagree and disintegrate.

Behold, how good and how pleasant it is for brethren to dwell together in unity!

It is like the precious ointment upon the head, that ran down upon the beard, even Aaron's beard: that went down to the skirts of his garments;

Psalm 133:1-2

It is a well-known fact that some of the believers who claim to be filled with the Holy Ghost and who anoint themselves with oil indiscriminately, are the most divided and confused groups one can find. Such groups end up this way because they erroneously seek the power of the Holy Ghost without cultivating the fruit of the Spirit. Like the Corinthians in Paul's time, they exercise spiritual gifts for fleshly gratification and not to glorify God. This notwithstanding, if we pay attention to the fruit of the Spirit through prayer and humility, the anointing produces amazing unity and harmony in the Body.

Unity in Spirit can only be fostered if it begins from the head and flows down. If the leader breeds bitterness and confusion, the same flows down to the rest of the body. In pharmacy, oil is used as the medium to hold many ingredients together by forming a suspension. The active ingredients in an oily suspension don't neutralise one another. The main ingredients don't subdue the less important ones. This is similar to the unity of the Spirit in the Church – believers don't neutralise one another and the imposing personalities don't quench the zeal of the weaker ones.

With all lowliness and meekness, with longsuffering, forbearing one another in love;

Endeavouring to keep the unity of the Spirit in the bond of peace.

There is one body, and one Spirit, even as ye are called in one hope of your calling;

One Lord, one faith, one baptism,

One God and Father of all, who is above all, and through all, and in you all.

Ephesians 4:2-6

Every Spirit-filled believer has his or her anointing with which he or she can influence others. The anointing is the oil of influence that gives us the power to lift others up. Job gave a detailed description of how he used the anointing on his life to edify others instead of causing conflict and discomfort among people.

When I washed my steps with butter, and the rock poured me out rivers of oil;

When I went out to the gate through the city, when I prepared my seat in the street!

The young men saw me, and hid themselves: and the aged arose, and stood up.

The princes refrained talking, and laid their hand on their mouth.

The nobles held their peace, and their tongue cleaved to the roof of their mouth.

When the ear heard me, then it blessed me; and when the eye saw me, it gave witness to me:

Because I delivered the poor that cried, and the fatherless, and him that had none to help him.

The blessing of him that was ready to perish came upon me: and I caused the widow's heart to sing for joy.

I put on righteousness, and it clothed me: my judgment was as a robe and a diadem.

I was eyes to the blind, and feet was I to the lame.

I was a father to the poor: and the cause which I knew not I searched out.

And I brake the jaws of the wicked, and plucked the spoil out of his teeth.

Then I said, I shall die in my nest, and I shall multiply my days as the sand.

My root was spread out by the waters, and the dew lay all night upon my branch.

My glory was fresh in me, and my bow was renewed in my hand.

Unto me men gave ear, and waited, and kept silence at my counsel.

After my words they spake not again; and my speech dropped upon them.

And they waited for me as for the rain; and they opened their mouth wide as for the latter rain.

If I laughed on them, they believed it not; and the light of my countenance they cast not down.

I chose out their way, and sat chief, and dwelt as a king in the army, as one that comforteth the mourners.

Job 29:6-25

Job's life sums up the influence of the anointing. It shows us what the anointing does in individuals and what it empowers them to do in other people's lives. The beauty of Job's anointing is the harmony between him and others. This harmony enabled him to have massive influence on those who needed the anointing. It is helpful to list the effects of the anointing on Job so that we can see what it produces in our lives. As the anointing comes upon us through the hearing of God's Word, prayer, anointing with oil, laying on of hands or acts of obedience, we should expect to see its manifestations as portrayed in Job's life.

- **Job washed his steps in butter and the rock poured rivers of oil to him:**

Washing your steps in butter represents washing your feet in the Word of God. Butter is obtained by churning milk, which represents the Word of God (1 Peter 2:2).

Verse 6 – *"When I washed my steps with butter, and the rock poured me out rivers of oil;"*

The Apostle Paul pointed the Ephesians to the cleansing effect of God's Word.

Husbands, love your wives, even as Christ also loved the church, and gave himself for it;
That he might sanctify and cleanse it with the washing of water by the word,
Ephesians 5:25-26

It is spiritually futile to pour volumes of anointing oil on yourself without the Word of God. The Word of God cleanses you for the application of the anointing just as you take a shower before you put body lotion on your body. To fail to obey the Word of God, but anoint yourself with oil is a vain exercise.

But it shall come to pass, if thou wilt not hearken unto the voice of the LORD thy God, to observe to do all his commandments and his statutes which I command thee this day;

that all these curses shall come upon thee, and overtake thee:

Thou shalt plant vineyards, and dress them, but shalt neither drink of the wine, nor gather the grapes; for the worms shall eat them.

Thou shalt have olive trees throughout all thy coasts, but thou shalt not anoint thyself with the oil; for thine olive shall cast his fruit.

Deuteronomy 28:15, 39-40

The conditionality for the anointing is doing God's will. Knowing and obeying the Word of God qualifies and positions you to receive the anointing because the Word directs you to do God's will.

Order my steps in thy word: and let not any iniquity have dominion over me.

Psalm 119:133

Job traced the source of the oil in his life to "the rock" – he said "the rock" poured him out rivers of oil. This "rock" is Jesus Christ who is the source of the anointing. The title "Christ" **(Christos)** is the Greek version of the Hebrew **Messiah** and it means "anointed." Jesus Christ is the "Anointed One" who anoints us to live victoriously and do the work of the ministry. Christ is the foundation on which the Church is built. The grace, power and life that sustain the Church come through having a revelation of Christ. Your life must be established on "the Rock" – Jesus Christ – before the anointing comes upon you. Anointing unbelieving persons destroys the sanctity of the anointing.

> *And I say also unto thee, That thou art Peter, and upon this rock I will build my church; and the gates of hell shall not prevail against it.*
>
> *Matthew 16:18*

- **Job went out to the gate and prepared his seat in the street:**

Job sat at the city gates where judicial issues were conducted and acted as a magistrate.

Verse 7 – *"When I went out to the gate through the city, when I prepared my seat in the street!"*

Believers are spiritual magistrates who are positioned at the gates of nations and cities to bind principalities and powers. The anointing empowers and positions you to bind the forces of evil and loose the blessings of God.

> *And I will give unto thee the keys of the kingdom of heaven: and whatsoever thou shalt bind on earth shall be bound in heaven: and whatsoever thou shalt loose on earth shall be loosed in heaven.*
>
> *Matthew 16:19*

Apart from binding and loosing things on earth, the Apostle Paul said believers will judge angels. If believers have the power to judge angels, it is obvious that they have the wisdom and power to settle disputes among people. There is too much confusion in the world and believers must take their positions at the gates and let peace and righteousness prevail.

> *Dare any of you, having a matter against another, go to law before the unjust, and not before the saints?*
>
> *Do ye not know that the saints shall judge the world? and if the world shall be judged by you, are ye unworthy to judge the smallest matters?*
>
> *Know ye not that we shall judge angels? how much more things that pertain to this life?*
>
> *If then ye have judgments of things pertaining to this life, set them to judge who are least esteemed in the church.*
>
> 1 Corinthians 6:1-4

- **Job commanded respect from the young, the old, princes and nobles because of the anointing on his life:**

People spoke well of Job because of the anointing on him. There are people who speak evil of anointed people no matter how good they are. However, others speak well of the anointing. Generally, the anointing brings respect and honour to those who have it.

Verses 8-10 – *"The young men saw me, and hid themselves: and the aged arose, and stood up.*

The princes refrained talking, and laid their hand on their mouth.

The nobles held their peace, and their tongue cleaved to the roof of their mouth."

• **Job delivered those who were oppressed:**

Job was anointed to deliver the oppressed. He was not anointed just for himself and his family. He delivered the poor that cried, and the fatherless, and helpless. The blessing of him that was ready to perish came upon him and he caused the widow's heart to sing for joy.

Verses 12-13 – *"Because I delivered the poor that cried, and the fatherless, and him that had none to help him.*

The blessing of him that was ready to perish came upon me: and I caused the widow's heart to sing for joy."

God anointed Jesus with the Holy Ghost and power to heal the oppressed.

How God anointed Jesus of Nazareth with the Holy Ghost and with power: who went about doing good, and healing all that were oppressed of the devil; for God was with him.

Acts 10:38

- **The anointing on Job made him a support to those who were incapacitated:**

Job was a righteous man with a sense of judgment that made him discern the needs of others and reach out to support them. Many people can't carry themselves and therefore need others to carry them. Anointed individuals believe for others and carry them on their faith.

Verses 14-17 – *"I put on righteousness, and it clothed me: my judgment was as a robe and a diadem.*

I was eyes to the blind, and feet was I to the lame.

I was a father to the poor: and the cause which I knew not I searched out.

And I brake the jaws of the wicked, and plucked the spoil out of his teeth."

Jesus Christ, the anointed Son of God, carried the sins of the world upon Himself.

Surely he hath borne our griefs, and carried

our sorrows: yet we did esteem him stricken, smitten of God, and afflicted.

But he was wounded for our transgressions, he was bruised for our iniquities: the chastisement of our peace was upon him; and with his stripes we are healed.

All we like sheep have gone astray; we have turned every one to his own way; and the LORD hath laid on him the iniquity of us all.

Isaiah 53:4-6

The world needs saviours who like Jesus will pay the price for others to be saved and delivered.

And saviours shall come up on mount Zion to judge the mount of Esau; and the kingdom shall be the LORD'S.

Obadiah 21

• **The anointing preserved Job:**

The devil attacked Job in many ways but the anointing kept him alive. He confessed that he would die in his own house and not perish in the open fields. He expected to live long and flourish like a tree under the dew. His glory was fresh and his strength was sustained.

Verses 18-20 – *"Then I said, I shall die in my nest, and I shall multiply my days as the sand.*

My root was spread out by the waters, and the dew lay all night upon my branch.

My glory was fresh in me, and my bow was renewed in my hand."

- **The anointing creates expectation:**

The anointing made people relate to Job with expectation. They knew that God had empowered him to bless them. Job's words had the power to give life like rain. He generated hope and inspiration in others through his leadership abilities. The inspirational leader comforted mourners.

Verse 21-25 – *"Unto me men gave ear, and waited, and kept silence at my counsel.*

After my words they spake not again; and my speech dropped upon them.

And they waited for me as for the rain; and they opened their mouth wide as for the latter rain.

If I laughed on them, they believed it not; and the light of my countenance they cast not down.

I chose out their way, and sat chief, and dwelt as a king in the army, as one that comforteth the mourners."

Job's life is a clear demonstration of the power of the anointing in someone's life. When you are symbolically anointed with oil, it is an opportunity to appropriate the actual power of the Holy Ghost. The anointing oil is a symbol of the Holy Ghost but it is not merely a physical substance. Its application has spiritual consequences and effects.

In concluding this book, I wish to remind us about some of the important things I covered. I explained that the anointing oil is not the Holy Ghost but a symbol of the Holy Ghost. In view of this, we should not overemphasise the anointing oil to the point where it takes the place of the Holy Ghost.

God commanded Moses to anoint Aaron, his sons, the Tabernacle and its instruments with the anointing oil. The anointing of people and things with oil separated them unto the Lord. In view of the power of the anointing oil, we have to apply the oil with decorum. The indiscriminate use of the anointing oil causes confusion in the Body of Christ. The anointing heals. It cleanses things and people who are unclean. It gives favour by imparting divine fragrance to believers. Through the anointing, God accepts sacrifices. The anointing is the fuel of the Holy Ghost that makes us shine with God's light. No believer is an island. Every believer lives for others and works for others. The anointing provides the environment for the harmonious functioning of believers.

Faith is the foundation of Christian living. If you believe that the Holy Ghost works with the anointing oil, He will release His power when you apply it. Believers who don't believe in the use of the anointing oil in New Testament Christianity are under no compulsion to use it. God does not need the application of oil to release His power. Those who believe in the use of the anointing oil must have a biblical revelation of the person of the Holy Ghost. It is the Holy Ghost who empowers believers to live victoriously – the oil is a symbol of the Holy Ghost. The anointing oil produces great impact on believers only when there is a perfect balance between the person of the Holy Ghost and the symbol of the anointing oil.

Let your head lack no ointment.

"Let thy garments be always white; and let thy head lack no ointment."

Ecclesiastes 9:8

LET BROTHERLY LOVE CONTINUE.

BOOKS BY AUTHOR